FIFTY WAYS TO PRACTICE VOCABULARY

Tips for ESL/EFL Students

BELINDA YOUNG-DAVY

WAYZGOOSE PRESS

Edited by Dorothy E. Zemach. Cover design by Maggie Sokolik.

Published in the United States by Wayzgoose Press.

CONTENTS

INTRODUCTION

Without grammar, you can't say much. Without vocabulary, you can't say anything.

It takes many hours to become proficient at anything—a sport, a hobby, a musical instrument, or a foreign language. Many thousands of hours, in fact! For a student of English, this can seem difficult to accomplish, especially if your only opportunity to study English is in the classroom.

This book will help you learn and practice vocabulary in English, both inside and outside the classroom. If you are already taking English classes, some of the tips will help you get more out of your classes. If you're not taking English classes—and even if you are—other tips will give you ideas to try on your own. Not every idea will work for every student. That's why there are fifty. We feel sure that many of the ideas presented here will bring you results if you try them sincerely.

Here is a suggested method for using this book:

1) Read through all of the fifty tips without stopping.

2) Read through the tips again. Choose five or six that you think might work for you. Decide when you will try them, and for how long.

3) Try to choose different types of ideas: some for learning new words, some for practicing and remembering words, some for using them. Also, choose some that you can practice with a friend or language learning partner, and some that you can do alone. For your convenience, the tips are divided by category: Finding and *Learning New Words, Flashcards, Practicing and Remembering Vocabulary,* and *Vocabulary Games.*

4) Each time you use one of the ways, make a note about how well it worked for you and why. Remember that most of the tips will work best if you practice them several times (or even make them a habit). Don't try a tip only once and decide it's no good for you. Give the tips you try a few chances, at least.

5) Every few weeks, read through the tips again, and choose some new ones. Discontinue using any methods that are not working for you.

The most important advice, though, is to actually *do* the suggestions you read about here. Wishing is not working. If you don't do the work, you won't see the results.

Finally, consider trying some of the other books in our *50 Ways to Practice* series. No one skill in English is really separate from the others. Speaking, listening, reading, writing, vocabulary, and grammar are all connected. Improving in one area will almost always bring improvements to other areas too.

❧ I ❧
FINDING AND LEARNING
NEW WORDS

❦ I ❦

MAKE GOOD CHOICES

Make a distinction between *active* vocabulary and *passive* vocabulary.

Active vocabulary includes words you need to be able to produce—such as for speaking or writing.

Passive vocabulary you only need to understand when you read or hear it.

It is normal to have a larger passive vocabulary than an active vocabulary, even in your native language.

When you choose words to study and learn, decide if you need to know them passively—just when you see/hear them —or whether you want to be able to use them actively in writing and speech.

Review and practice active vocabulary more often than passive vocabulary. And remind yourself that it's okay not to learn every word in the English language!

2

LOOK A WORD UP TWICE

Two times is more than twice as good as one!

When you want to learn a new word, especially for your active vocabulary, try this system.

First, use a bilingual dictionary to look up the word and get a general idea of the meaning.

Next, look the word up in an English-only dictionary. An English-only dictionary will give you a more specific definition and idiomatic usages. It will also show grammatically accurate and useful example sentences. This will show you how to use the word in addition to just the meaning.

You can find both bilingual dictionaries and English-only dictionaries free online.

❦ 3 ❦

USE TECHNOLOGY

Use an online dictionary with a pronunciation feature when you look up a new word.

Practice the pronunciation a few times by saying the word out loud.

You can also find pronunciation demonstrations for many words on YouTube—just type (for example) "pronounce establishment" to hear some examples. You can choose British English or American English pronunciation.

Even if you will be reading English more than speaking it, knowing a word's pronunciation will help you learn and remember that word.

❧ 4 ❧

USE VISUAL CUES

To increase your vocabulary, use a magazine.

Choose a magazine with many pictures in it (even an adver-
tisement works well for this). Pick a page and label every
object in the picture in English. Look up any words you
don't know in a dictionary.

You can also photocopy the page and label the photocopy.
Then use the unlabeled picture to 'test' yourself later.

5

ORGANIZE

Use an organization system to help you learn and review your vocabulary.

Keep an English vocabulary notebook with you at all times.

Write down new words that you see in advertisements; read in a book or magazine; or hear spoken by teachers, friends, on TV, etc. Check the spelling of words that you hear. Add the meanings from a bilingual dictionary or an English-only dictionary—whatever you find most useful.

Every day, go through the notebook and decide which words are the most useful. Then study those words. It's okay to cross out words that aren't really useful for your life.

❧ 6 ❧

IMPROVE ACADEMIC VOCABULARY

If your goal is to improve your academic vocabulary, you can use one of the Academic Word List (AWL) websites on the Internet to learn and practice academic vocabulary such as

http://www.victoria.ac.nz/lals/resources/academicwordlist

The AWL contains lists of words that are used in university lectures in English-speaking countries. The vocabulary is arranged in sublists. Sublist 1 contains the most frequently used words; sublist 2 contains the next most frequently used words, and so on.

There are also online websites with exercises for practicing words on the AWL such as

http://www.englishvocabularyexercises.com/AWL

❧ 7 ❧

WRITE EXAMPLES

Remember the phrase "Use it or lose it!" That means if you don't use your new words, you will probably forget them.

When you learn a new word or phrase, write three sentences for each: one sentence from a dictionary and two sentences of your own.

If you have a hard time writing original sentences, it's probably because you do not really understand what the word means or how it works. Check some different online dictionaries to get some more examples, or search for examples of your word or phrase online.

See if you can use your new word when you write letters, emails, or social media posts. Try to use your new word when you speak, too.

❧ 8 ❧

CREATE A PICTURE DICTIONARY

Go through magazines and look for pictures of objects or actions related to vocabulary words. Look for pictures to represent verbs, adjectives, and adverbs, not just nouns.

If you don't have access to any magazines, you can print images from web pages.

Consider grouping words for one topic together – for example, vocabulary of objects found in the kitchen, or words to describe a farm. This is an especially good way to learn vocabulary words for your personal hobby or interest.

Remember to re-read your dictionary from time to time, to help you remember the words you've learned.

❧ 9 ❧

LEARN EXPRESSIONS AND PHRASES

Learning expressions and phrases, and not just single words, increases your ability to understand native speakers.

When you read, notice which words are used together. You can also pick up phrases when you listen to English conversations and media.

The free website ESL Gold has a section for vocabulary words and phrases, divided by level and then by topic:

https://eslgold.com/build-vocabulary/words-phrases/

You can also learn idioms using online idiom websites. Here is one, from Dave's ESL Café:

http://www.eslcafe.com/idioms

This YouTube channel shares "one-minute English" videos of useful expressions with explanations:

https://www.youtube.com/@lexicallab9848/videos

USE PREFIXES

A prefix is part of a word that comes at the beginning of the word. Pay attention to prefixes when you learn vocabulary; these show meaning. Here are just a few examples:

- a- or an- : not. *apolitical, anarchy*
- co-: together. *coworker, coordinate*
- con- with. *conversation, conjunction*
- inter-: between. *interstate, interview*
- micro-: small. *microphone, microscope*
- mid-: half or middle. *midterm, midnight*
- pre-: before. *prefix, preschool*
- re- To do something again. *rewrite, review*
- sub-: below. *subway, submarine*

Of course, not every word that begins with these letters is using a prefix. *inter-* in the word *intervening* is a prefix; but not in the word *interesting*. If you can't tell if something is a real prefix, check a dictionary.

Learning and recognizing prefixes will help you remember the meaning of words that you look up. It can also help you guess the meaning of new words. For example, *il-* means 'not,' as in *illegal* (not legal). What do you think *illogical* means?

❧ II ❧

USE SUFFIXES

A suffix is part of a words that comes at the end. Pay attention to suffixes when you learn vocabulary; these show parts of speech.

For example, the suffix *-ly* usually means a word is an adverb. When you see or hear a word ending in *-ly*, you know it is probably an adverb.

Moreover, as you learn new nouns, you can quickly check dictionary to see if *-ly* can be added to them to make an adverb. It's an easy way to increase your vocabulary.

When you are speaking, and you don't know the correct word form, you can guess by adding a common suffix. You won't always guess correctly, but sometimes you will—and even if you guess wrong, the other person will probably know what you mean.

Here are some common suffixes:

- -able/-ible (adjective; *capable, edible*)
- -al (adjective; *frugal, diagonal*)
- -ance/-ence (noun: *science; maintenance*)
- -ate (verb; *conjugate, regulate*)
- -en (verb; *quicken, soften*)
- -ment (noun; *government, punishment*)
- -tion (noun; *nation, portion*)
- -ward (adverb; *toward, backward*)

As you saw with prefixes in tip #10, not every word that ends with these letters has a genuine suffix. *Hyphenate* is a verb; but *fate* is a noun. If you are not sure, check a dictionary.

❧ 12 ❧

LEARN COLLOCATIONS

When you learn new words, pay attention to the other words in the sentence. *Collocations* are words that often are used together.

Prepositions are often used in collocations with verbs. For example, the verb *concentrate* is often followed by the preposition *on* + a noun, such as in the sentence, *It was hard to* **concentrate on** *the teacher's lecture today.*

Many dictionaries will list common collocations for nouns and verbs.

When you write words into your vocabulary notebook or make flashcards, list one or two common collocations in addition to the single word. This will help you use your new word correctly, not just recognize it when you read or hear it again.

13

READ ENGLISH AS OFTEN AS POSSIBLE

Reading is important for several reasons.

First, it will help you remember vocabulary you already know. If you learn a word one day and then never see it or use it again, you will probably forget it.

Reading is a wonderful way to notice collocations (see tip #12).

You will meet new words when you read; if they seem important, look them up and write them down.

Reading will help you see how words you mostly know are used naturally.

What should you read? Anything!

There are special "graded readers" made specially for learners of English. Here is one list:

https://wayzgoosepress.com/readers/

You can choose books YA books (for "young adult") that will be simple in concept but still have a lot of useful vocabulary, or choose a book you have read in your own language to read again in English.

Commit to reading a short story on a website or short magazine or newspaper articles in English every day.

❧ 14 ❧

USE A THESAURUS

To increase your vocabulary quickly, use a thesaurus—a dictionary of *synonyms* (words that have the same or a similar meaning).

Once you have learned a word very well, it is a good idea to look it up in a thesaurus to look for synonyms for your word. Pick one or two synonyms to learn.

You can try Longman's Language Activator, which you can buy, or you can use a free online thesaurus, such as the one here:

https://www.thesaurus.com/

You can often find paper copies of thesauruses in used bookstores. Even ones that are several years old are still very useful and interesting.

❧ 15 ❧

LEARN SYNONYMS

Check the meanings of synonyms in a dictionary to see if there are any differences in how the words are used.

Is one word more formal and another more informal? Does one have a more positive meaning, and one a more negative meaning?

For example, to describe a thin person, *skinny* is negative, *slim* is positive, and *lithe* is more formal or literary.

Different synonyms are used in collocations, too. For example, in English we say *a little old lady* and not *a small old lady*, even though *little* and *small* mean the same thing. Using the correct synonym will make your English sound more natural.

FOCUS ON WORD GROUPS

After reading an article or story in your own language, underline 10 description words or 10 verbs and look them up in English. Pay attention to any differences in the way they are used.

You can even focus on word groups before you read! For example, imagine you want to learn vocabulary for your hobby, horseback riding.

First, think of ten words in your own language that you think are useful (such as *mare*, *stable*, *saddle*, *bridle*, *reins*, *mount*, *canter*, and so on).

Then look up those words in English.

Finally, search for an article online about your topic. As you read the article, see how many of your words are mentioned. Then read one or two more articles. Could you find all your words?

LEARN A WORD EVERY DAY

Join an ESL word-of-the-day website.

Some online ESL vocabulary websites teach a new vocabulary word every day. You can learn the meaning of the word, listen to the pronunciation, and do some practice exercises.

Here is an examples:

www.englishwithjo.com/category/esl-word-of-the-day/

This is a site for native and fluent speakers, but it is still useful for learners:

https://www.merriam-webster.com/word-of-the-day/calendar

Some stores also sell "word of the day" desk calendars. That's 365 new words for you every year!

❧ II ❧
FLASHCARDS

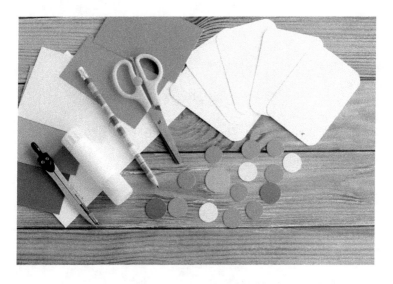

Flashcards are a convenient and effective way to study and practice vocabulary. Here are some different ways of making and using them.

❧ 18 ❧

MAKE SIMPLE FLASHCARDS

To learn and remember words, make flashcards.

Write the vocabulary word on one side. Draw or cut out a picture of the object or action and put it on the other side. Practice a word like this:

1. Look at the picture side and think of the word in English.
2. Say the word out loud.
3. Spell the word—spell it out loud, or write it down.
4. Turn the flash card over to see if you are correct.

If you are correct, put the card in a "finished" pile. If you make a mistake, try again with the same card in a few minutes.

Review your flashcards (even the ones you get right) every few days.

MAKE FULL FLASHCARDS

On one side of the card, draw a simple picture (or cut out a picture and glue it on). On the other side, write:

- The word and part of speech
- The definition
- One or two sentences using that word (from the book or website where you found the word, or your dictionary).
- If possible, some different word forms and collocations
- Any important notes

Practice with a friend. Your friend holds all the cards, shows you the pictures one at a time, and asks you these questions:

- What's this?
- How do you spell it?
- What does it mean?

- Can you use it in a sentence?
- What are some other forms of the word?
- What are some expressions with this word?

Even if your friend doesn't know your words, he/she can still check the answers by reading the word side of the card.

Example for the adjective *patient*:

Side A (picture only)

Word: patient (adj) [pronounced like: p<u>ay</u>-shent]

Definition: able to wait without being upset or complaining

Sentence: He isn't very patient. He can't wait five minutes.

Other forms: patience (n); patiently (adv); impatient (adj; opposite)

Collocations: to be patient; to have patience; wait patiently

Important: Not the same as "patient," noun = person who visits a doctor or dentist!

Side B (word and information)

LEARN DIFFERENT WORD FORMS

If your word is a noun, write both the singular and the plural form of the word on the flashcard. This is especially important if the plural is irregular (*tooth; teeth*).

If your word is a verb, write the present, past, and participle forms of the verb (*cry, cried, crying, has cried*).

You can also write words in the same word family—that is, different parts of speech (*usual, usually, unusual; regular, regularly, regulate, regulation*).

❧ 21 ❧

LEARN WITH OTHERS

Use a free online flash card website such as this one:

http://quizlet.com

This website lets you download flashcards other people have made, as well as create your own to share. Quilt is free for students and is also available as an app.

Brainscape is another great program. It works on computers, tablets, and smartphones. You can create your own flashcards and share them with others. The program will also review the most difficult words for you more often.

There is both a free version and a paid version, but for most independent students, the free version is good enough. Find Brainscape here:

http://brainscape.com

❧ 22 ❧

CATEGORIZE BY SHAPE OR COLOR

Make differently shaped cards for different parts of speech. For example, make

- square cards for verbs
- triangle cards for nouns
- round cards for adjectives and adverbs
- rectangle cards for conjunctions (*and*, *but*, *so*) and subordinators (*while*, *as*, *because*)

This allows you to study and review specific parts of speech. This is very helpful when studying for vocabulary tests.

You can also use different colors instead of different shapes. Use different colors of paper to make flashcards for different parts of speech, or write the words in a different color.

❧ 23 ❧

USE TIME WISELY

Carry some flashcards with you every day. Whenever you have a few minutes free, go through some of your flash cards or have a friend test you.

This is a good way to efficiently use time on the bus or train, waiting for appointments, or just before your class begins.

If you use a flashcard app on your phone (see tip #21), you will almost always have your flashcards with you! Remember that it is easier to make study a habit if you do a little bit every day, instead of a long session every few weeks. You will make faster progress that way too.

❧ 24 ❧
REVIEW OFTEN

Review at least 10 vocabulary words from the previous month every month by checking your flashcards and then making a new sentence for each word. Write the sentences down.

If possible, have a fluent English speaker check your new sentences to make sure they are correct.

If that isn't possible, check the sentences in a dictionary or online (just search for your word), and write new sentences by changing just a few words from the original. This will still help you learn.

❧ III ❧
PRACTICING AND REMEMBERING VOCABULARY

25

SET REASONABLE GOALS

Many students try to learn too many vocabulary words at one time (perhaps just before an important test?).

However, if you try to learn 30 words every week, you will probably remember the meaning of only 10-20 words from each week by the end of the month. Also, you won't be able to learn the definition, spelling, and pronunciation of 30 words in addition to when and how to use those words correctly, all in one week.

Set a realistic goal, such as learning 5-10 new words every week. Learn a few words well, instead of many words badly.

✿ 26 ✿

CONNECT THE 'NEW' TO THE 'KNOWN'

When you learn a new word, find ways to connect it to things you do everyday, your hobbies, or things you know a lot about.

For example, if you have just learned the word *decisive*, write it or say it in sentences about important choices or strong decisions you have made recently. This will help you remember the word and how to use it.

If you have trouble using new words in conversations, you can write a few sentences or a short paragraph in a diary or journal. Writing words down helps you to remember them.

❧ 27 ❧

CREATE RELATED WORD FORM
GRIDS

To really learn a word family, fill in a chart with two forms
of the words to start (for example, noun and adjective), and
practice using those forms. Two or three weeks later, fill in
the other two forms (for example, verb and adverb).

NOUN	VERB	ADJECTIVE	ADVERB
identity identification	identify	identifiable	identifiably

A word family with four forms

You might need to check a dictionary to find some forms, if
they are a little different from the main noun.

strength	strengthen	strong	strongly

A word family with some different spellings

Write any interesting or important information into the chart. Note that some words will not have all four forms.

refusal *not refuse, which means garbage!*	refuse	(none)	(none)

❧ 28 ❧

CREATE A SYNONYMS AND ANTONYMS GRID

Synonyms are words that have similar a similar meaning. *Antonyms* have the opposite meaning.

If there is a word you commonly use, it will probably be useful for you to learn related words.

WORD	SYNONYMS	ANTONYMS
large	huge; enormous	little; small; tiny
funny	amusing; humorous	sad; serious

To find synonyms and antonyms, check a dictionary or thesaurus. This online thesaurus gives both synonyms and antonyms for words that you search for:

http://thesaurus.com

USE DIFFERENT REVIEW METHODS

Using words in different ways will help you remember them better.

For example, look for your word when you read, say your word out loud (either in conversation or just to yourself), and write your word in a sentence.

Review verbs every week using a different kind of sentence. For example, the first week, use the verb in two affirmative sentences. The next week, use it in two questions. The next week, use it in two negative sentences. In addition, use different verb tenses as well.

❧ 30 ❧

ESTABLISH A STUDY TIME

Make a specific time for vocabulary learning or practice each week.

For example, you can review vocabulary words for 15 minutes each day just before you go to bed, or for 5 minutes every morning before you get out of bed, or while you eat breakfast.

If your life is already busy, see if you can find any "unused" time. Can you check flashcards while sitting on the bus or train? Can you play simple English podcasts or songs while you are driving or doing chores at home?

❧ 31 ❧

COMBINE SKILLS

Find a picture in a magazine. Write a story or a detailed description about the picture. Before you begin, decide about how many nouns, verbs, adjectives, and adverbs you will use. Look up any new words you need to complete your story.

When you are finished, record your story or description on your smartphone to practice pronunciation.

Finally, listen to your recording a few days or even a few weeks later, to see if you can recognize your words when you hear them and remember their meanings.

❧ 32 ❧

TAKE DICTATION

Have a friend read a short paragraph in English to you, repeating each sentence two or more times. Write down the sentences. Compare your dictation with the paragraph after you have finished.

Gradually increase the length of the paragraphs you use.

You can also do this by yourself, using a song or short conversations in movie or television clips you find on YouTube (many of which have a "closed caption" feature, or CC, that shows the words). Many smartphones and other devices have a "text to speech" function that will read a book or document to you.

❧ 33 ❧

DO A DICTOGLOSS

This is similar to a dictation, except you do not write anything down while you are listening.

Have a friend read a short paragraph to you two or more times. After you have listened to the paragraph several times, write down a summary of it. Then compare it with the original.

As with dictation (see tip #32), you can use a talk on YouTube or the text-to-speech function of your device to read you something if you do not have a friend who can do this with you.

❦ 34 ❦

USE RHYMES

Find short poem or fun song in English that uses rhymes. Memorize the poem or song and recite it for your friends and family. This will help improve your pronunciation as well as increasing your vocabulary.

Some good authors to look for include Dr. Seuss, Shel Silverstein, and Ogden Nash.

For slightly longer and higher-level poems, try Robert Louis Stevenson. Check the bottom of this webpage to find a good selection:

https://www.poetryfoundation.org/poets/robert-louis-stevenson

❧ 35 ❧

WRITE IT DOWN

Copy a short paragraph from a textbook, a newspaper, or magazine (either by hand or on the computer—some experts though feel that writing by hand is a better way to memorize information). Leave out the words that you want to practice by writing a blank _____ instead of the word. (Be careful not to leave out too many words, though!)

Several days or a week later, try to complete the paragraph by writing the correct words in. Pay attention to spelling.

Then compare it to the original to see how you did.

❧ 36 ☙

MAKE YOUR OWN TEST

For a greater a challenge, copy a paragraph in your textbook or a short article in English. Leave out every 6th word (with more than 4 letters in it). Study those words. Fill it in a few days later. Pay attention to spelling.

If you have a friend who is studying English too, you can make tests for each other. These don't have to be friends in your same class—you can easily exchange tests with people you know online. Then you can each check and grade each other's tests. Why not have a fun weekly competition?

CREATE A WORD WEB

A word web helps you remember new vocabulary and how to use it by linking new words to other words you already know.

For example, imagine you are learning the word *athlete*. First write the word *athlete* in the middle of a piece of paper, and draw a circle around it. Next, think of a word that is associated with *athlete*, such as *sports*. Write the word and draw a circle around it. Draw a line to connect it to *athlete*.

Continue as in this example:

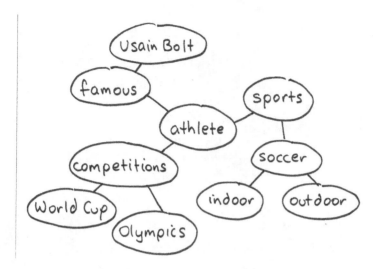

Then try to make sentences using the word *athlete* and the words in the word web.

Usain Bolt is a famous athlete who competed in the Olympics.

❧ 38 ❧

SAY IT

Even if you do not have English-speaking friends to talk with, you can practice your vocabulary words out loud.

Do this as often as possible; for example, in you can practice when you are alone in the house, walking to school, or in the shower.

Saying words out loud not only helps you remember the word but also improves your pronunciation.

Can you make up a song with your words, or sing them to a familiar tune? I remember in junior high school memorizing a long list of English prepositions by singing them to the tune of the children's song "Pop Goes the Weasel."

You can easily find versions of "Pop Goes the Weasel" online if you would like to learn this catchy tune!

USE SOCIAL MEDIA

Writing is a great way to practice using new vocabulary. Use new words you have learned in posts on your Facebook page, on Twitter, on Instagram (tag us with @wayzgoose-press to show off your efforts!), or when you text friends who speak English.

If you don't have many English-speaking friends, you can write bilingual posts, so you are not excluding anybody.

If you feel brave, why not record yourself saying something in English, or reading a simple poem, and then post the video to TikTok or as a reel on Instagram or Facebook?

40
READ

Reading English is one of the best ways to practice vocabulary.

Read news articles online, and buy English newspapers and magazines. Notice words that you have already learned to see how those words are used by native speakers. Pay special attention to collocations.

If you can, read aloud to practice pronunciation—especially word stress. This will help you move words from your passive vocabulary to your active vocabulary.

Many publishers sell "graded readers" for people learning English. They have books at many different levels. Wayzgoose Press has books for beginners up to high intermediate, in both ebook and print. You can find our books here:

https://wayzgoosepress.com/readers/

There are also several services that advertise free ebooks every day. Here are some of them:

http://freebooksy.com

http://thefussylibrarian.com

These are books for fluent English readers, of course, so they might be a little challenging for you. But many ebook readers have built-in dictionaries, so you can easily check vocabulary as you are reading.

DEVELOP LISTENING SKILLS

Listen to English to improve your vocabulary. Watching YouTube videos is a fun way to learn new vocabulary in context and recognize words that you are learning. You can also look for TED Talks on topics that you are interested in.

http://www.ted.com

You can also watch TV shows on streaming services. Even if this seems difficult at first, it will get easier over time as you learn the different characters and the way they talk. You can also watch most shows with English subtitles, so you can see and hear the words at the same time.

Why not try a podcast? Listen while you are walking, exercising, or doing chores. Here is a site that lists lots and lots of different podcasts:

https://www.podbean.com/

❧ 42 ❧

CREATE ROLE PLAYS WITH FRIENDS

Rewrite conversations from your textbook with a few of your classmates, using new vocabulary you want to practice.

Practice several times, and then perform the role play for other classmates.

You can also write your own original role plays about something fun or exciting that you have done or want to do.

You can choose to write out every word and then memorize your parts, or just decide what is happening and then make up dialogue each time as you go along.

❧ 43 ❧

LOOK FOR NEW INFORMATION

Twice a month, go through all of your vocabulary cards or flashcards and look for words with similar meanings.

Look up all of the words with a similar meaning again in two different dictionaries to see if the definitions have any differences.

Pay special attention to the example sentences; look differences in usage. For example, the verbs *study* and *learn* have a similar meaning, but are used in different ways.

🐝 44 🐝

ACT IT OUT

Research has shown that there is a connection between the body and the mind that can help you learn and remember.

When you are learning a new word, see if you can associate an action with it. This is easier to do with verbs and adverbs, of course, but is still possible with verbs and nouns.

For example, imagine you want to learn and remember the word *veterinarian* (often called a *vet*, for short). Can you act out an injured animal, like a dog with a hurt leg? And then a person taking care of that dog? Repeat those actions several times, as you say *vet — veterinarian — vet* to yourself, either out loud or in your head.

People who follow exercise videos or take exercise classes in English learn that vocabulary very easily and very well!

❧ 45 ❧

TAKE A BREAK

This may sound counterintuitive (new word? look it up!), but sometimes the best thing you can do for your independent learning is to take a break. You don't want to "learn" to dislike English, or to dislike studying.

If you are feeling discouraged or tired or burned out or frustrated, take a day or two off. Relax with some friends or listen to music or spend some time outdoors. Take a hot shower or bath. Go for a walk or visit a park. Plants and trees, as well as water (lakes, rivers, or the ocean) can lift your spirits, as can sun on your skin.

Here: Enjoy these relaxing scenes!

❧ IV ❧
VOCABULARY GAMES

❦ 46 ❦

MAKE A CONCENTRATION GAME

Make and play a Concentration game! You can play with a friend, a group, or even alone. (Sometimes this game is called Memory.)

1. Cut 30 squares of paper (or use 30 cards). Divide the cards into two groups of 15.
2. Write one vocabulary word on one side of a group of 15 cards. On the other 15 cards, write the definition.
3. Mix up each group of 15 cards separately.
4. Lay the first group of 15 cards face down, in 5 rows of 3 cards.
5. Then lay down the second group of 15 cards, also in 5 rows of 3 cards.
6. Pick up a card from the first group. Say the word out loud.
7. Pick up a definition from the second group. Read it out loud.
8. If they match, take the two cards out of the game.

If they don't, put them back, face down, and select two new cards.

9. Continue until all the cards match. It's important to say the word and the definition out loud each time! This is what helps you learn and remember them.

Variations: For a longer game, start with 40 cards, and divide them into two groups of 20. You can also match synonyms, antonyms, words in the same word families (nouns and adjectives, for example), or words and "cloze" sentences (sentences that use the word, but with a ___ instead of the word).

❧ 47 ❧

PLAY BINGO

Play Word Bingo with three or more classmates or friends. One player will be the caller. Choose twenty-four words all of you want to review. Each player draws a bingo card and decides where to fill in the spaces with the twenty-four words. The caller will write a list of definitions (or sentences; or synonyms, etc.) for the twenty-four practice words. When the caller reads a definition from the list, all of the players have to find and mark the correct word on their bingo cards. Do not let other players see your card. The first person who is able to mark five words in a straight or diagonal row says *Bingo!* The caller checks to see if all of the words are correct. If they are correct, the player has won; if all of the words are not correct, everyone continues playing.

A sample Bingo card:

B	**I**	**N**	**G**	**O**
rapid	relevant	patience	tangerine	fate
deceive	mixture	oddly	falcon	pick
poverty	scarce	**Free Space**	hopeful	dour
hint	hastily	among	astound	barely
unrest	meanwhile	moose	beyond	listless

PLAY WORD SCRAMBLE

Play Word Scramble with classmates or friends. Each person cuts twenty squares of paper and writes one word on each square.

Each person writes:

- a name on 2 or 3 squares
- verbs on 4 or 5 squares
- nouns on 4 or 5 squares
- adjectives or adverbs on 2 or 3 squares
- conjunctions (*and, or, so, but*) on the rest of the squares.

All of the squares are placed faced down on the table and mixed up. Each person selects four squares and the group tries to make some sentences using those words. Put squares that cannot be used face down and mix them with the other squares. Continue playing until you have used as many squares as possible.

You can also play Word Scramble by yourself, by choosing words at random from your noun, verb, adjective, and adverb flash cards to write on at least twenty squares.

❧ 49 ❧

PLAY CHARADES

Play Word Charades with classmates or friends.

Each person writes 5 nouns, 5 verbs, and 5 idioms on a piece of paper. Do not show your list to anyone.

Each person takes a turn silently acting out a word or idiom from his or her list.

Other players have to guess the word or idiom. The person who can guess the most words is the winner—although you don't really need to have a "winner" to enjoy playing charades.

At the end, show your lists to each other and explain any vocabulary words that other member of the group did not know.

DO WORD PUZZLES

In addition to playing word games, word puzzles are an excellent way to practice vocabulary and spelling.

Go online to find free English puzzle-maker websites such as

http://www.discoveryeducation.com/free-puzzlemaker

Recently, the game Wordle has become very popular. It is easy to play, and you can play free once a day. The rules are easy—you just need to guess a five-letter word in English. But you only have six chances!

Find the game (and the rules—click on the question mark in the upper right-hand corner) here:

https://www.nytimes.com/games/wordle/index.html

BONUS TIP!

LOOK AT LOTS OF EXAMPLES

If you want to find a lot of example sentences for your new vocabulary, use a word concordance website—these gather many, many real-life examples of how words are used and show them to you.

Here is one for language leaners:

https://www.sketchengine.eu/skell/

And here is a more general one, the Virtual Language Centre:

http://vlc.polyu.edu.hk/concordance/

Pay attention to word order, collocations, and the punctuation in the sentences.

AFTERWORD

Learning another language is never fast, but the *Fifty Ways to Practice* series will speed things up by showing you how to practice more efficiently and effectively, both inside and outside the classroom. It is useful for beginning through advanced levels. The *Fifty Ways to Practice* series offers short, practical guides to different areas of English language study for motivated students.

Note: We have priced these *Fifty Ways to Practice* guides very cheaply, because we want education and learning to be available to as many people as possible. However, our authors are highly qualified professionals who work hard to create these books. If these books are useful to you, please recommend them to your friends—but please do not share them freely. Our authors will continue to write excellent and cheap books for you if they make a little money. That way, we all win. Thank you for your support!

If you have comments or suggestions (such as ideas for future books that you would find useful), feel free to contact the publisher at editor@wayzgoosepress.com, check out the offerings on our publishing website at http://wayzgoosepress.com, or join us on Facebook.

To be notified about the release of new 50 Ways titles, as well as other new titles and special contests, events, and sales from Wayzgoose Press, please sign up for our mailing list. (We send email infrequently, and you can unsubscribe at any time.)